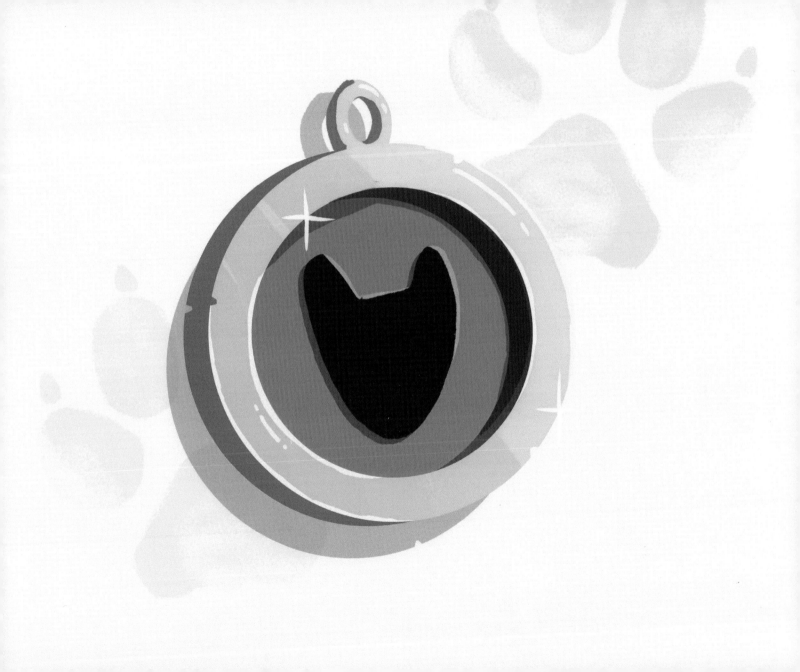

Scout's Journal

Camping checklist

Before we go camping I have to make sure we have everything we need.

Tent

Food

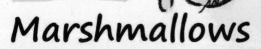
Marshmallows

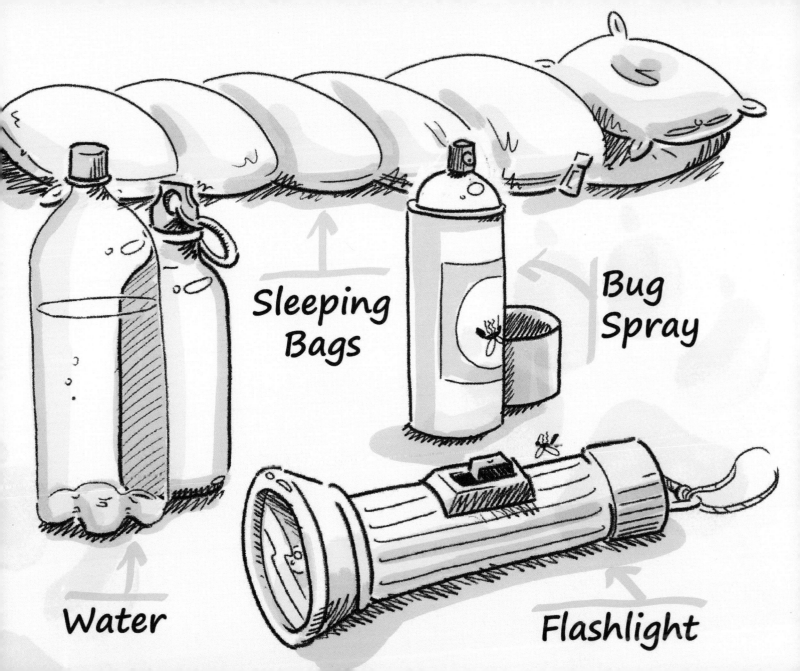

Sleeping
Bags

Bug
Spray

Water

Flashlight

This looks like
a super fun place to camp!
While Joe and Will set up
the tent I need to make
sure the campsite is safe.

I'll move the tent over here so a dead tree branch doesn't fall on our tent!

Scout's Journal

There are so many wonderful things to see in the forest. I like to draw pictures of all of the animals I have discovered.

Mouse

Deer

Raccoon

This one will steal your food!

Beaver

Great builder

Spider

Rabbit

Hide and seek is a perfect camping game. There are so many places to hide.

1... 2... 3...

Emerald will never find me here.

Scout's Journal

FUN CAMPING GAMES

Counting stars

Skipping rocks

Cloud watching

Tic
Tac
Toe

Pine cones   Rocks

One of the best things about camping is the campfire but a tiny spark could start a forest fire if it lands on these dry leaves and twigs.

Before Joe starts the fire I need to move this dry brush far away from where the fire will be.

Now the fire is safe for cooking hotdogs, melting marshmallows and sharing spooky stories with family.

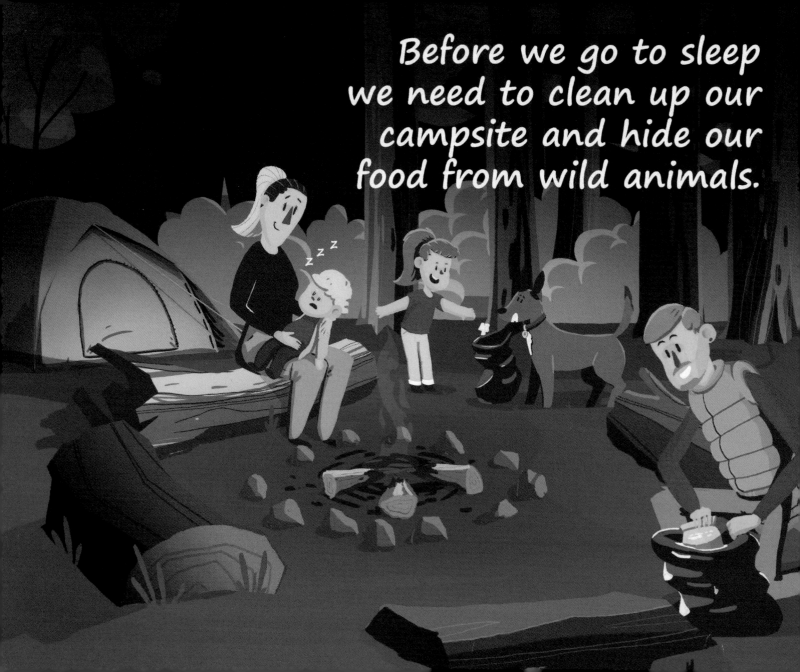

If we don't hang our food up in this tree raccoons might steal it or a bear might visit our camp looking for a snack.

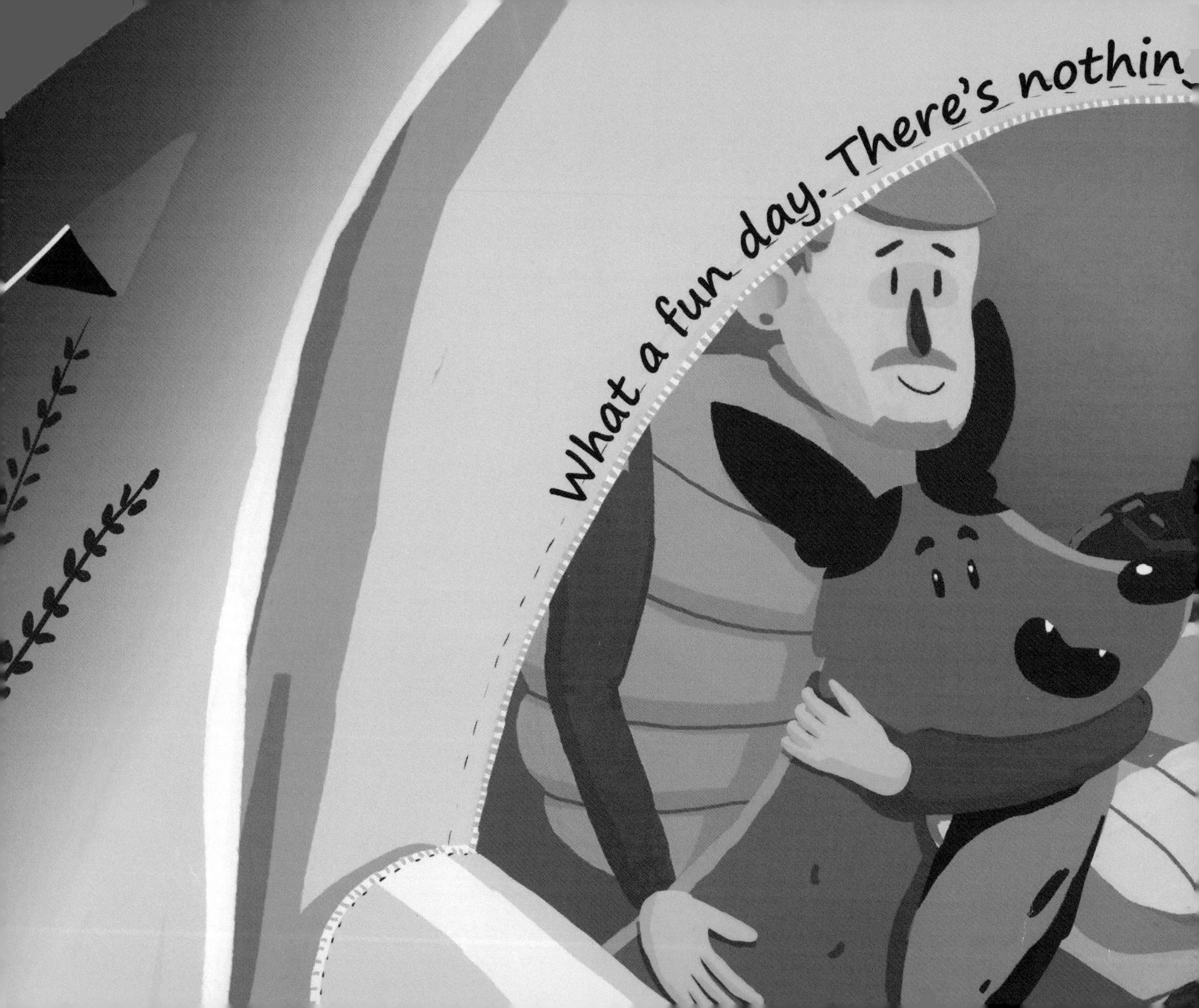

What a fun day. There's nothin

love more than camping.

Credits

Illustrated by
Piotr Ciereszyński

Written by
Scout's Best Friend, Joe Robinet